AF481682

Woolly Can

Written by Yakira

Illustrated by Glen Henry

This book is dedicated to my daughter Sarayah, who has a fascination with goats.

Woolly can **dance**.

Woolly can
swing.

Woolly can **jump** over the jungle gym.

Woolly can
drink.

Woolly can **eat** all the
mangoes and leaves
with a bleat.

Woolly can **walk**.

Woolly can
stray.

Woolly can **play**
in the sun all day.

Woolly can **bathe**.

Woolly can **snuggle**
in her tiny bed
made of hay and rubble.

10 Facts about Goats

A baby goat is called a kid.

Goats are happy in herds and not as pets.

They are one of the cleanest animals.

Goats are very intelligent and curious.

They communicate with each other by bleating.

Goats are not fond of water.

They have four stomachs.

Goats are very good climbers.

They are picky eaters.

Goats have excellent night vision.

Thank you, Glen for doing the illustrations to my satisfaction.

Thank you JerryLee, for kickstarting the uploading process and Alene for completing it.

Thanks to my husband and family members for their support and encouragement.

Thank you, mom for taking care of your dear granddaughter so that I could focus on my book.

Thank you, aunt Merna for guiding me through the writing process.

Most of all, thank you God for your grace and mercy.